MEDIATION FOR LITTLE PEACEMAKERS

Working It Out Together

For Grades 3-6

by Max Nass, M.S. & Marcia Nass

Mediation for Little Peacemakers
by Max Nass, M.S. & Marcia Nass

Published by:
The Center for Applied Psychology, Inc.
P. O. Box 61587
King of Prussia, PA 19406 U.S.A.
Tel. 610/277-4020

The Center for Applied Psychology, Inc. is the publisher of Childswork/Childsplay, a catalog of products for mental health professionals, teachers and parents who wish to help children with their developmental, social and emotional growth.

All rights reserved. The Center for Applied Psychology, Inc. grants limited permission for the copying of "Mediator Handbook Sheets" and items located in Appendix I, II, and III from this publication to its customers for their individual professional use. Permission for publication or any other use must be obtained in writing from The Center for Applied Psychology, Inc., P.O. Box 61587, King of Prussia, PA 19406.

Copyright ©1996 by The Center for Applied Psychology, Inc.
Printed in the United States of America.

ISBN 1-882732-42-1

ACKNOWLEDGMENTS

We are most gratefully indebted to all the teachers and young mediators who piloted this program and whose feedback made invaluable contributions in making this curriculum possible.

Special thanks to elementary school teachers Garnetta Thomas, Linda Berg, Phil Gibson, Enid Deale, Louise Coleman, Rita Friedman, Alice Scott, Lisa Petker and Gloria Cunny.

To all the young mediators, thank you for working hard to create more peaceful classrooms and ultimately a better world for us all.

TABLE OF CONTENTS

INTRODUCTION

Preface 1
Why Teach Mediation 3
How It Began 4
How to Fit Mediation Into Your Curriculum 4
Starting Up the Program 5
Session by Session Breakdown..6
An Overview of How It All Comes Together 7
What You'll Need to Get Started..8

PART 1: READY, SET, GO

Session #1
Preliminary Peace Lesson..10
Mediator Background 11
Creating "My Mediator Handbook" 12
Qualities of Mediators 13
"My Mediator Handbook" Sheet #1 - Mediator Qualities 14

Session #2
Good Listening Skills 16
"My Mediator Handbook" Sheet #2 - Good Listening Ideas 17
Mediator Facts 18
"My Mediator Handbook" Sheet #3 - Ten Key Facts About Mediators 19
Brainstorming..20
"My Mediator Handbook" Sheet #4 - Steps to Brainstorming..............................22
"My Mediator Handbook" Sheet #5 - Journal Page 23

Session #3
Repeating (Paraphrasing)...25
Cooling Off (Anger Management Skills) 26
"My Mediator Handbook" Sheet #6 - "Cool It" Suggestions.................................28
The Mediator Script 29
Mediator Rap Song Lyrics 31
Teachers Notes on the Mediator Script...32
Mediator Clue Cards 33
"My Mediator Handbook" Sheet #7 - Mediator Clues...34

PART II: ROLE-PLAYING: PRACTICE MAKES PERFECT

Session #4
Role-playing: Maximizing Its Effectiveness..36
Conflict Examples 39

Session #5
Mediator Suggestions 41
"My Mediator Handbook" Sheet #8 - Mediator Suggestions......................43

Session #6
Handling Objectives 47
"My Mediator Handbook" Sheet #9 - Handling Objections 48

Session #7
Mediator's Discipline 50

Session #8
Mediator Quiz 52
Picking the Mediators 53
How to Enhance the Program..53
How Other School Personnel Can Help 54

PART III: GETTING PARENTS INVOLVED

Bringing Mediation and Conflict Resolution Home 56
De-stressing Tips for Parents..57
De-Stressing Common Sense 58
Help! My Kids Are Driving Me Crazy!..59
Cool-Off Zones 60
Anger Management Activities 61

APPENDIX 1

Why I Want to Be a Classroom Mediator..64
Teacher's Report Card..65
Mediator Certificate..66
Mediator Schedule..67

APPENDIX 2

Mediator's Classroom Conflict Report Form 70
Preliminary Parent Letter 71
Parent Letter: Congratulating Mediators 72

APPENDIX 3

50 Sample Role-Plays for Mediation 74

About the Authors 77

PREFACE

Welcome to *Mediation for Little Peacemakers: Working It Out Together.* This manual is for teachers as well as community leaders who want to train elementary school students in the art of mediation. The ideas in this manual have been tested and confirm that children as young as eight can learn these invaluable life skills and have fun simultaneously.

Not long ago, The American Psychological Association recommended that by teaching children conflict resolution and mediation skills, the tide of violence in our country can be slowed or even reversed. The APA recommends beginning this training at the elementary school level, when children's minds are the most impressionable, and we can make a difference that can last a lifetime.

Mediation for Little Peacemakers provides a step-by-step framework for training an entire class or group as mediators. As each skill is introduced, students will actively begin role-playing these new ideas as they learn how to peacefully reconcile differences.

The curriculum consists of easy-to-follow lessons which teach problem-solving, active-listening, role-playing and brainstorming. Reproducible masters make it fun for kids to create their own "Mediator Handbook." "The Mediator Rap" song helps students memorize "The Mediator Script," which is one of the three essential components in teaching them to become mediators. There are also plenty of tips for teachers to facilitate classroom discussions and make the experience fun for everyone.

Every lesson is presented in a hands-on "workshop format" to engage children and get them actively involved. Your role as a teacher of mediation is to become more of a "trainer" and "facilitator" than "lecturer–" introducing your students to these skills and then stepping back and enabling them to make their own discoveries, observations, and conclusions.

Mediation for Little Peacemakers gives you the framework, but ultimately it is your faith in your students that will make this program a success.

WHY TEACH MEDIATION?

Conflict is a way of life and something we cannot avoid. From the time we are very young, we have conflicts about who is sitting next to whom, who goes first, and who gets the bigger piece of cake. Thousands of surveys confirm that children are influenced by the countless television shows (including cartoons) that encourage fighting, name-calling or other uncooperative behavior as means of solving a conflict. By teaching children mediation skills at an early age, we demonstrate creative and constructive ways to handle conflicts, and empower them for a lifetime.

How many times have you heard:
> *"Kevin hit me"*
> *"Janet took my toy"*
> *"Lamar got in front of me"*
> *"Andy stepped on my toe"*
> *"Beth called me a nasty name"*

As you know, many of these "everyday conflicts" take time and energy away from learning and having a good time at school. Often they try the patience of even the most seasoned teacher. Objectives and goals for the day are put on hold as "time out" is taken to help resolve daily disagreements, often one right after the other. But there is an alternative. That alternative is called mediation.

A classroom Mediator is a student who has been trained to help his peers resolve a problem and arrive at a peaceful solution. Classroom Mediators work in pairs and are highly effective in helping their classmates solve non-physical disagreements through a series of simple steps that you can teach them.

The decision to train your young students takes time and energy, but consider it an investment. After you get the classroom mediation program underway, you will begin giving some "everyday problems" to the classroom Mediators on duty. As the program progresses throughout the year, you will be amazed at how many problems can be simply solved by the classroom Mediators.

There are other advantages too: 1) The young Mediators gain self-esteem and leadership skills and give other children in the class strong peer role models; 2) overall communication skills in the classroom improve as you develop a more cooperative classroom environment; and 3) the children bring these skills with them into their homes and communities, often teaching their parents and family members. A perfect example of this is a young Mediator named Randy.

One afternoon, after school, Randy's mother was having a very loud argument on the phone with the telephone company over a bill. Randy picked up an extension and asked, "Would you like a mediator to help you solve the problem?" At first both adults were shocked, but Randy led them through the mediation process to a peaceful solution to which both his mother and the phone representative agreed. Countless other mediators have reported using these skills to help relatives and friends in their homes and communities settle differences peacefully.

Lastly, you will be giving your students a very precious gift: a foundation that will allow them not to resort to guns or physical violence as a means to solving problems as they grow up and become teenagers and our country's future citizens and leaders.

How It Began

Mediation for Little Peacemakers grew out of a need at my own school to teach mediation skills to young people. I began training students in classrooms where teachers were open and receptive. Through word of mouth about the success at my own school, I was asked to conduct workshops for teachers, parents, and community leaders. After speaking with teachers and principals, I discovered that many schools (often those that can use it the most) simply could not afford school-wide mediation programs and "experts" to train their faculties and students. *Mediation for Little Peacemakers* was developed specifically for teachers who want to begin using these ideas to train their students and create classrooms where a higher caliber of learning can take place.

You do not need to have a school-based program. You do not need any previous exposure to mediation or conflict resolution methods or skills. All you need is the commitment to the time it will take and faith in your students to give this program wings.

Mediation for Little Peacemakers is flexible. As the person who knows your students the best, you can improvise and bring your own creativity to the program. Over time, as you work with different groups of children, you will be learning how to become a "mediation expert." As an old proverb says, we are all teachers and students of each other, and sometimes, as you know, our young students turn out to be our greatest teachers.

How to Fit Mediation Into Your Curriculum

You can make mediation a separate lesson or part of a Language Arts (English) or Social Studies program:

1. Language Arts: Through mediation, children learn how to express themselves in more positive ways. They learn how to articulate their feelings, become good listeners, and summarize what they are hearing through paraphrasing (also known as repeating). In addition, they are developing brainstorming and problem-solving skills they will carry with them for the rest of their lives.

As children read novels (for class or enjoyment), you might ask them to become aware of any conflicts the characters are experiencing in the stories. Have them think about how the characters might resolve their conflicts through conflict resolution and mediation principles.

2. Social Studies: Through mediation, children learn interpersonal skills and how to relate to others. Often Mediators gain self-esteem and leadership roles. They learn how to work together as a team with a common goal: the betterment of their class and society as a whole.

When studying different periods of history, you might want to ask students how the skills of mediation might have prevented people from hurting one another, attacking each other, taking people's land and possessions, and getting revenge.

Children will begin to see that getting along with others is like a thread woven through all areas of life.

STARTING UP THE PROGRAM

Mediation for Little Peacemakers is an easy, step-by-step approach for training your students as Mediators. Not all children will become classroom Mediators. Only students who are (1) well behaved, (2) good listeners, and (3) able to memorize The Mediator Script will become your classroom Mediators; however by training all students as Mediators, you will be giving your entire class the skills and awareness to seek creative responses to conflict. There have even been reports where the most disruptive student turns around and becomes a successful Mediator—gaining attention from helping rather than hurting others. Teachers tell me that sometimes they are surprised to discover who turns out to be their best Mediator.

The training period takes eight weeks, broken down into eight simple sessions. This gives the children time to learn and practice their new-found skills before tackling additional ones. Since each skill builds on the preceding one, it is important to follow the lessons in order. As students are learning each new skill, they will simultaneously be practicing those in which they've already become proficient and gaining more confidence in themselves.

Teach one session each week, preferably at the beginning of the week, with a quick review (time permitting) later in the week. After going over The Mediator Script and Mediator Rap in Session #3, it is most important to review the script with the class every day. The easiest way of doing this is to play the tape and have the class rap along. Also, as part of their homework, the students can study The Mediator Script.

You may want to begin each additional session with a quick review of the preceding lesson and always end it by asking: "Are there any questions?" (Children should be encouraged to ask questions.)

As the weeks progress, you will be creating a sense of purpose among all the children which will give them the impetus to solve many conflicts on their own. You may want to ask the children from time to time to share their successes, including those from home, as they begin to incorporate many of these ideas into their lives both in and out of school.

A session-by-session breakdown appears on the following pages.

SESSION BY SESSION BREAKDOWN

Session 1   Peace Lesson   15 min.
                   Background of Mediators   5 min.
                   Qualities of Mediators   5 min.
                   Creating the Mediator Handbook   5 min.

Session 2   Good Listening Skills   10 min.
                   Mediator Facts   10 min.
                   Brainstorming   10 min.

Session 3   Repeating (Paraphrasing)   5 min.
                   Cooling Off   5 min.
                   The Mediator Script   10 min.
                   Mediator Rap Song   5 min.
                   Mediator Clue Cards   5 min.

Session 4   Role-playing with Conflict Cases 30 min.

Session 5   Mediator Suggestions   10 min.
                   Role-playing   20 min.

Session 6   Role-playing   20 min.
                   Handling Objectives   10 min.

Session 7   Role-playing   25 min.
                   Mediator Discipline   5 min.

Session 8   Mediator Quiz   20 min.
                   Picking the Mediators   10 min.

AN OVERVIEW OF HOW IT ALL COMES TOGETHER

Let's look at a typical classroom day.

You are teaching a lesson in science. Your back is to the children. Somewhere in a corner of the classroom, you hear two of your students involved in a loud argument. For the purposes of the illustration, let's call them Ethan and Janice. Ethan screams out, "That's my pencil." And Janice yells back, "No, it's mine."

You ask Ethan and Janice (called Problem Kids) if they would like the Mediator's help in solving the problem. You check your Mediator schedule (posted in front of the room) and see Carlos and Mei Ling are the Mediators on duty for that day.

You ask Carlos and Mei Ling to help Ethan and Janice solve their problem. (It will usually take between five or ten minutes to solve a classroom problem.)

The four students (two Mediators and two Problem Kids) proceed to a quiet place. The Mediators ask the Problem Kids to agree to four basic rules (which they will learn in the mediator script.)

1. Do you both agree to try and solve the problem?
2. Do you both agree not to interrupt?
3. Do you both agree not to call each other names?
4. Do you both agree to tell the truth?

After each rule, both Problem Kids say "yes." The Mediators then lead them through the step-by-step approach where both children tell their side of the story. The Mediators listen closely and repeat (usually summarizing) what each Problem Kid has said. Then they very simply ask: "What can you say or do to solve your part of the problem?" Both Problem Kids make suggestions. (If they cannot do this, the Mediators make suggestions, which is part of the training they receive.) A few moments later, a peaceful decision is reached. (They will flip a coin for who gets the pencil.) Both Mediators ask each Problem Kid respectively, "What would you do if the problem happens again?" The Problem Kids work out what they will do. The Mediators congratulate them for solving their problem peacefully and shake their hands. Everyone agrees not to discuss the problem with friends to prevent rumors from spreading.

The Mediators report to you that the problem has been solved. In almost all daily classroom disagreements, the problem can be solved with the classroom Mediators on duty, but there are some exceptions that will necessitate your involvement. They include:

1) If there's a weapon;

2) If the Mediators have tried and one or both kids can't or won't solve their problem;

3) If one of the Problem Kids has made a threat against a Mediator.

WHAT YOU'LL NEED TO GET STARTED

Mediation requires a quiet place to work out the problem. Many teachers take a corner in the back of the room and make it the "Mediator Corner." They put tables and chairs for the mediation in the corner and the rules for solving a problem on a nearby bulletin board. Others prefer "A Magic Mediation Carpet," a nice-sized rug where the children can sit and go through the mediation process. Still others prefer the children to use the hallway right outside the door (in your view, where you can see them through the window in the door) for absolute peace and quiet.

PART I: READY, SET, GO

SESSION #1

Preliminary Peace Lesson

Mediator Background

Creating "My Mediator Handbook"

Qualities of Mediators

PRELIMINARY PEACE LESSON

OBJECTIVE: To teach children that, as human beings, we will always have conflicts, but we have a choice in how we handle these conflicts. Violence is never the answer.

MATERIALS: blackboard, chalk.

WARM-UP: Go around the room and ask, "Why is physical fighting bad?" Write the answers on board. (Tip: Could get hurt, could get killed, person could get their bigger brother or sister after you, could get suspended from school.) Ask: "Why do people physically fight?" (Tip: Think it makes them look powerful; to feel like a winner; to take their bad feelings out on someone else; if they don't fight, others will think they look like a wimp.) Discuss positive and negatives. (Tip: You can bring up the NBA, where in basketball you get thrown out of the game if you physically fight.) Discuss how really strong people don't need to prove anything by fighting.

PROCEDURES: 1. Ask the class: "What is a conflict?" (Tip: When people disagree about something.) Explain: Conflicts aren't good or bad, but we can handle them in good or bad ways. Ask: "Has anyone here had a recent conflict? What happened? How did you solve it? How would you do it differently?"

2. Have two students come to the front of the room to role-play an interview. Tell them they should pretend they are on the news. One is the reporter, and the other one is the important person being interviewed. Write these questions on the blackboard: "What is your favorite television show?" "How do the people on the show solve problems?" "Do they physically fight?" "Who is your hero?" (Can be a celebrity or real person.) How does that person solve his or her problems? What is a "real hero?" (A person who uses his or her brains and not a fist or a weapon to solve a problem.)

OPTIONAL: Break children into groups of two and have one play the reporter and the other the person being interviewed using the above questions. They can reverse roles if time allows.

SHARING: Have children go home and interview a family member about his or her hero and how that person solves his or her problems.

MEDIATOR BACKGROUND

OBJECTIVE: To teach children what a mediator is, and to introduce the concept of Mediators as helpers and heros.

MATERIALS: Folders, felt-tip pens for Mediator Handbooks (see page 12, Creating "My Mediator Handbook.")

WARM-UP: Distribute folders, pens, and fasteners for folders. Ask students to write their names on the cover of the handbook and "MY MEDIATOR HANDBOOK."

EXPLANATION: Explain that the class will be starting a new and exciting program called *Mediation for Little Peacemakers*.

PROCEDURES: 1. Ask: "Who knows what a Mediator is?" (Tip: A Mediator is a person who helps kids solve a problem without fighting.) Ask: "How are some ways you help people at school? At home?" Write all ideas on the blackboard.

2. Ask: "What are some other fun names we could give the Mediators?" (Tip: Peace Force, Mediator Rangers, Peace Team, Super Mediators, Peace Rangers.)

3. Ask: "How are Mediators heroes? How many of you would like to be Mediators?" Ask: "What do you think the Mediators in our classroom will do?" (Tip: Help kids in our class solve problems.) Tell the class: "Over the next few weeks, we will be learning all about Mediators–our special helpers and heroes."

SHARING: Tell children to go home and share with a family member what they are learning about Mediators.

OPTIONAL: You can send a letter home to parents/guardians to let them know you are starting a new program that will be encouraging children to seek peaceful solutions to conflicts. **Parent's Letter (Appendix III) can be photocopied and sent out.**

CREATING "MY MEDIATOR HANDBOOK"

As you hand out the reproducible sheets from the curriculum, the children will place them in their special folders.

For each child: Take two pieces of oak tag cut into 8 1/2 x 11" sheets.

Three-hole punch oak tag cover and all pages.

Hand out folders and fasteners.

Show children how to put fasteners through holes.

Tell them every paper they receive should go into their Mediator Handbook.

QUALITIES OF MEDIATORS

OBJECTIVE: For children to learn the qualities of Mediators.

MATERIALS: Blackboard, "My Mediator Handbook" Sheet #1 - Mediator Qualities.

WARM-UP: Have children write down what they think some of the qualities of Mediators are.

PROCEDURES
1. Ask the class: "What are the three qualities of Mediators?" Write these answers on the blackboard. After each one is listed, ask why that quality is important.

   The qualities are:
   A. Well behaved. (Tip: Must show other students the right behavior to set a good example.)

   B. Good listener. (Tip: To understand the problem and be able to explain it to all students involved.)

   C. Ability to memorize The Mediator Script. (Tip: Knowing the script by heart helps the Mediator to solve problems faster and easier.)

EXPLANATION: Explain that The Mediator Script is a series of steps the Mediator goes through to help solve a problem.

2. Make two columns on the blackboard: "Mediators Are," "Mediators Are Not." Children should write their ideas on the sheets. Ask for suggestions. Children should fill them in on their handbook sheets.

MEDIATORS ARE:

Well-behaved kids
Good listeners
Able to keep mediation secret
Able to memorize the mediator script
Able to not take sides
Kind
Helpers and heroes

MEDIATORS ARE NOT:

Bullies
Fighters
Police people
Name-callers
Troublemakers
Bossy
Mean

"MY MEDIATOR HANDBOOK" SHEET #1
MEDIATOR QUALITIES

MEDIATORS ARE:

_____

_____

_____

_____

_____

_____

MEDIATORS ARE NOT:

_____

_____

_____

_____

_____

_____

SESSION #2:

Good Listening Skills

Mediator Facts

Brainstorming

GOOD LISTENING SKILLS

OBJECTIVE: To teach children active listening skills and why it is important to be a good listener when you are a classroom Mediator.

MATERIALS: "My Mediator Handbook" Sheet #2 - Good Listening Ideas.

WARM-UP: Tell the class you will read a story aloud, and while you are reading, you want everyone to talk to the person next to him or her. Read for two minutes. Then ask questions about the story: "What was it about? Who was the main character? Was anyone able to understand what I saying?"

PROCEDURE: 1. Have two students come to the front of the room. One will be the poor listener. The other student will tell what (s)he is doing after school today. The exercise should take 30 seconds. (Choose a talkative child to be the speaker.) You might want to whisper to the poor listener what (s)he should do. The poor listener can pretend (s)he (1) looks at his/her watch, (2) ties his/her shoe, (3) calls to a friend nearby, (4) yawns, (5) sings, (6) dances around, (7) constantly interrupts, etc.

Have the children freeze. Ask the class: "How do you think the person felt while telling the story?" Ask the class: "What does a bad listener do?"

2. Repeat the exercise with two more children. Now, one will be a good listener and the other will describe what (s)he would do if (s)he won a million dollars in the lottery (all the places to go, things to buy, people (s)he would help, etc.). You may want to whisper to the good listener what (s)he should do. The good listener demonstrates (1) eye contact, (2) nodding his/her head, (3) paying attention, (4) none of the poor listeners traits. Ask the class: "How do you think the person telling the story feels?"

3. Hand out "My Mediator Handbook" Sheet #2. Have the children write down the things good listeners do. Review. Write on board. Have children copy. (Tips: make eye contact, smile or nod, pay attention, do not interrupt.)

SHARING: Have the children go home and practice really listening to a family member.

MY MEDIATOR HANDBOOK SHEET #2
GOOD LISTENING IDEAS

Some ideas for being a good listener:

1. _____

2. _____

3. _____

4. _____

MEDIATOR FACTS

OBJECTIVE: For children to become familiar with the beliefs and responsibilities of Mediators.

MATERIALS: "My Mediator Handbook" Sheet #3 - Key Facts About Mediators.

WARM-UP: Ask the class: "In what situations do you think Mediators would not get involved in a mediation?" [When two children are physically fighting and the fight is not broken up; if a weapon is involved (run and get an adult); if one or both kids do not want to solve the problem; if one or both kids will not cool off their hot temper(s); if a Mediator is best friends with a Problem Kid (can't be neutral).]

PROCEDURES: 1. Hand out the Mediator Handbook Sheet #3. Go around the classroom and have children take turns reading. Stop and discuss or ask if there are any questions.

SHARING: Have the children go home and share what they are learning with a family member about Mediators. Ask them to review the 10 facts.

MY MEDIATOR HANDBOOK SHEET #3
10 KEY FACTS ABOUT MEDIATORS

The 10 Key Facts About Mediators:

1. Mediators are well-behaved so other students will respect them and listen to them.

2. Mediators believe students want to solve their problems.

3. Mediators believe conflicts can be settled without fighting.

4. Mediators can help students solve problems in most cases without the help of the teacher.

5. Mediators on duty do not break up fights because they might get hurt or become involved. Mediators are not police officers. If there is a fight, a Mediator will ask other kids to break it up.

6. When both kids are angry, Mediators help them cool off BEFORE they try to solve the problem. When they are calm, Mediators ask either one to speak first. Mediators always ask the angriest kid to speak first, so that (s)he doesn't interrupt.

7. Mediators NEVER force the Problem Kids to solve their problem. If either student does not want to solve his or her problem with the Mediator, (s)he is taken to the teacher or an adult.

8. Mediators do not take sides. If one of the Problem Kids is a Mediator's best friend, (s)he should tell the teacher to pick another Mediator.

9. Mediators let the Problem Kids come up with *their own solution* to a problem. If the Problem Kids cannot find a solution, the Mediators can offer suggestions with the Problem Kids' permission. (We will go over this later in Mediator Suggestions.)

10. If a Mediator gets in a fight, (s)he can lose his or her job.

BRAINSTORMING

OBJECTIVE: To teach kids how to creatively problem-solve through a special skill called Brainstorming.

MATERIALS: "My Mediator Handbook" Sheet #4 and #5 - Brainstorming and Journal Page.

EXPLANATION: "Mediators sometimes need to offer suggestions to help Problem Kids to come up with solutions to their problem. Mediators brainstorm to come up with suggestions. Brainstorming is like a game with rules."

WARM-UP: Ask children if they can list the rules for Brainstorming. Write them on the board.

THE RULES FOR BRAINSTORMING ARE:

1. All ideas are good.
2. No one is allowed to say good or bad things about your idea.
3. Say silly things just to come up with ideas.
4. Use other people's ideas to come up with new ones.
5. Come up with as many ideas as possible.

PROCEDURES: 1. Hand out "My Mediator Handbook" Sheet #4. Play The Brainstorming Game: Hold up an object and ask the children to brainstorm how many things they can do with this object. You can break the class into two different teams like a game show if desired. Give them one minute for each object. Get out your watch and say, "GO."

Objects include: paper clip, scotch tape, magic marker, sock, hat, toothpick. (Tips for paper clip: make necklace, clean nails, pick a lock, use for counting, in place of a button, clip a piece of paper, make an art design.)

2. Now brainstorm ways to solve a problem. Have children make up problems, real or imagined.

BRAINSTORMING ACTIVITY:

NASA calls you up and says it is inviting you to go to the moon with a group of astronauts. You can pick four people from your class to go with you. They will leave the decision up to you. You don't know who to choose or what standards to base the decision upon. Your teacher tells you to brainstorm some ways to decide. (Tip: Pick on the basis of who is the bravest, most athletic, smartest, nicest person to be around, just pick my best friends, draw straws so no one is mad at me.) Have kids make up some of their own creative stories to brainstorm.

SHARING: Share what you learned about brainstorming with a family member. Tell the children, "The next time you have a problem, brainstorm some ways to solve it." Write your solution in "My Mediator Handbook" Sheet #5 - Journal Page.

MY MEDIATOR HANDBOOK SHEET #4
BRAINSTORMING

The rules for Brainstorming are:

1. All ideas are good.
2. No one is allowed to say good or bad things about your idea.
3. Say silly things just to come up with ideas.
4. Use other people's ideas to come up with new ones.
5. Come up with as many ideas as possible.

Brainstorming Ideas

_____
_____
_____
_____
_____

MY MEDIATOR HANDBOOK SHEET #5
JOURNAL PAGE

I had a problem.

The problem was: _____

_____

_____

_____

It was with: _____

_____

_____

I brainstormed many ideas. Some of them were: _____

_____

_____

This is the one I picked to solve my problem: _____

_____

_____

_____

Check one:

___ It worked. Yeah! My problem is solved.

___ It didn't work.

___ I had to try something else. This is what I tried: _____

_____

_____

_____

SESSION #3

Repeating (Paraphrasing)

Cooling Off

The Mediator Script

The Mediator Rap

REPEATING

Note to Teachers: Repeating is also known as paraphrasing, but young children understand the word "repeating" better.

OBJECTIVE: To teach children how to listen carefully and then repeat in their own words what they just heard.

MATERIALS: Repeating Examples for Teachers (below).

WARM-UP: Go around the room and have each student tell about the happiest time they can remember. The person next to him or her should repeat (by summarizing) what the first student said and then say the happiest time he or she can remember. (Tell children to keep it short: one sentence.)

EXPLANATION: Tell the class: "In mediation, after a Problem Kid tells his or her side of the story, the Mediator will repeat in his or her own words what the Problem Kid said. We are going to try some examples."

PROCEDURE: 1. Tell the class: "I will pretend to be the Problem Kid and you will pretend to be the Mediator. I will say something, and you will repeat it in your own words."

REPEATING EXAMPLES FOR TEACHERS:

"I was walking down the stairs and Ronald pushed me." (Tip: "You said Ronald pushed you when you were walking down the stairs?")

"We were playing in the gym and Anthony grabbed the ball from me." (Tip: "So you're saying Anthony grabbed the ball from you in gym?")

"Mary took my pencil off my desk when I wasn't looking." (Tip: "So, Mary took a pencil off your desk?")

"Susan called my mother a 'jerk' and then I hit her." (Tip: "You're saying you hit Susan because she called your mother a name?")

"John borrowed a quarter from me last week and hasn't paid me back." (Tip: "So you're saying John hasn't paid you back the money he owes you?")

"Brenda knocked my coat down in the closet and didn't pick it up." (Tip: "Brenda knocked your coat down and didn't pick it up? Is that what you're saying?")

2. Have children make up some suggestions. One child pretends to be the Problem Kid. The other child pretends to be the Mediator, repeating what the Problem Kid said. Call a few groups to the front of the room.

SHARING: Have the children go home and practice repeating with a family member.

COOLING OFF

OBJECTIVE: To teach children that Mediators cannot help Problem Kids solve their conflict until they are cooled off.

MATERIALS: "My Mediator Handbook" Sheet #6 - Cool It Suggestions.

EXPLANATION: Tell the class: "People cannot solve their problems when they are very angry. First, they have to cool off. Our temper is like a slice of pizza. We wouldn't take a bite out of the pizza if it was steaming hot out of the oven. Our tempers are the same way. We have to let them cool off first before we can solve our problems."

WARM-UP: Go around the room and ask kids to tell one way they cool off when they are angry. Write suggestions on the board. (Only positive ones.)

PROCEDURES: 1. Hand out "My Mediator Handbook" Sheet #6. Have children write down ways to cool off.

2. Ask the children the following questions about cooling off as it relates to mediation:

COOLING OFF QUESTIONS:

1. "What does it mean to cool off?" (Tip: To calm down and be ready to solve your problems instead of wanting to hurt someone.)

2. "Why is it important to cool off?" (Tip: Because you can't solve a problem if you are thinking about getting even with someone.)

3. "If two children are trying to solve a problem with two Mediators, why would the Mediators want them to be cooled off?" (Tip: So it would be easier to solve the problem.)

4. "What could happen if they didn't cool off?" (Tip: They might interrupt each other when talking and they might even start fighting with one another.)

5. "If one of the Problem Kids isn't cooled off, what do you do if you are a Mediator?" (Tip: Wait until he or she calms down.)

6. "What are some suggestions a Mediator can give a Problem Kid to cool off?" (Tip: Take deep breaths, go to the girl's or boy's room and put some cold water on your face, count to 10, close your eyes and imagine a peaceful place, take a few sips of cold water from the water fountain.)

7. "If a Problem Kid doesn't cool off, what should the Mediator do?" (Tip: One of the Mediators should tell the teacher.)

**Note to Teachers: The more you know about how each student cools off, the easier it will be to get him or her to calm down when (s)he is angry. If one of the Problem Kids is very angry, tell him or her to stay in the classroom while the other Problem Kid goes out in the hallway or in the back of the class with the classroom Mediators. Give the hot-tempered child a chance to cool off before sending him or her to begin solving the problem.

SHARING: Have the children go home and interview a family member on how he or she cools off when angry.

MY MEDIATOR HANDBOOK SHEET #6
"COOL IT" SUGGESTIONS

Here are some ideas to cool off hot tempers. Mediators give these suggestions to Problem Kids when they are very angry.

1. Count to 10 (or even 100).

2. Think of a happy time in your life.

3. Drink a glass of cold water.

4. _____

5. _____

6. _____

7. _____

8. _____

9. _____

10. _____

THE MEDIATOR SCRIPT

OBJECTIVE: For children to understand what The Mediator Script is and the importance of memorizing the script.

MATERIALS: "My Mediator Handbook" Sheet #7 - Mediator Clues, Mediator Rap Lyrics.

EXPLANATION: Tell the class: "We are now going to be learning a very important part of becoming a Mediator. You cannot become a Mediator unless you know The Mediator Script by heart. A rap song, The Mediator Rap, is going to help us learn the song."

WARM-UP: Play The Mediator Rap. Ask the children what they think The Mediator Script is. (It is a series of questions Mediators ask to help the Problem Kids solve their problems.)

PROCEDURES:
1. Give a copy of The Mediator Script to each child. Go around the room and have each child read a line. You might want to divide the class into two groups: Mediator 1 and Mediator 2. Have the two groups take turns reading their parts.

2. Have some kids come up to the front of the class as "rappers" and rap along with the children on the cassette.

SHARING: Tell the children: "Go home and practice The Mediator Script. You can 'rap it' for a family member."

Note to Teachers: During this week, you should spend five minutes every day going over The Mediator Script with The Mediator Rap lyrics.

THE MEDIATOR SCRIPT

Mediator 1: Hi, my name is _____ and I'm a Mediator.

Mediator 2: Hi, my name is _____ and I'm a Mediator.

Mediator 1: Do you both agree to try and **solve** the problem?

Mediator 2: Do you both agree not to **interrupt?**

Mediator 1: Do you both agree not to call each other **names?**

Mediator 2: Do you both agree to tell the **truth?**

Mediator 1: **What happened** (1st person)? Repeat.

Mediator 2: What happened (2nd person)? Repeat.

Mediator 1: What can you say or do (1st person) to **solve** your part of the problem? Would this **solve** the problem **for you** (2nd person)?

Mediator 2: What can you say or do (2nd person) to solve your part of the problem? Would this solve the problem for you (1st person)?

Mediator 1: What can you do **differently** (1st person) if the problem happens again?

Mediator 2: What can you do differently (2nd person) if the problem happens again?

Mediator 1: Do you **both agree** that the problem has been solved?

Mediator 2: **Tell your friends** that the problem has been solved so they stop talking about it. Congratulations on solving your problem!

THE MEDIATOR RAP LYRICS

Do you both agree to try and solve your problem?

Do you both agree not to interrupt?

Do you both agree not to call each other names?

Do you both agree to tell the truth?

What happened? (Repeat)

What happened? (Repeat)

What can you say or do to solve your part of the problem?

Would this solve the problem for you?

What can you say or do to solve your part of the problem?

Would this solve the problem for you?

What can you do differently if the problem happens again?

What can you do differently if the problem happens again?

Do you both agree that the problem has been solved?

Tell your friends that the problem has been solved so they stop talking about it.

Congratulations on solving your problem!

TEACHER'S NOTES ON THE MEDIATOR SCRIPT

1. Mediators 1 and 2 are interchangeable. Children must learn all parts of the script.

2. Both Problem Kids must agree to the four rules or the mediation will not work:

   a. Try to solve the problem
   b. Not to interrupt
   c. Not to call each other names
   d. Tell the truth

If a student does not want to agree to one of the rules, the Mediators might ask why he or she objects. The children usually agree when they talk it out.

3. Remind the Mediators to ask the Problem Kids their names before beginning the mediation. Also remind them to always ask the angriest Problem Kid what happened first; otherwise, the angriest person may interrupt.

4. Remind the Mediators to repeat what a Problem Kid says. This is an important part of using good listening skills for everyone.

5. When the Mediators ask: "What can you say or do to solve your part of the problem?" we are trying to focus on what the person who is answering the question can do him or herself to solve the problem. (e.g., "I'll say I'm sorry, or I'll stop bothering him.")

Many times the children will say what the other person can do when asked this question. (e.g., "If he stops bothering me, or if he says he is sorry.") This is not correct; however, we accept this answer if it is the only way the children can make peace.

6. When a child gives a solution, the other child should agree. If there is no agreement, the child who gave the solution should come up with another solution. If (s)he can't, the Mediator should ask the other child to suggest a solution. Finally, Mediators offer solutions with the Problem Kids' permission.

7. Remind the Mediators to ask what can be done differently if the problem happens again. This question helps the children think about the consequences of their actions.

8. Both children must agree the problem has been solved. If not, Mediators are reminded to look for alternative solutions.

9. Remind the Mediators to tell the Problem Kids to tell their friends that the problem has been solved, so they stop talking about it. Most of the time the other kids involved are told that the Mediators have helped to solve the problem.

THE SCRIPT *MUST* BE MEMORIZED FOR A CHILD TO BECOME A MEDIATOR.

MEDIATOR CLUE CARDS

The Mediator Clue Cards have key words or phrases which help children to learn the Mediator Script. You can photocopy the reproducible page and give it to students. If you'd like, you can take a large piece of oak tag and write the clues on it and then hang it in a prominent spot so the children can easily see the clues.

MY MEDIATOR HANDBOOK SHEET #7
MEDIATOR CLUES

Hi, my name is _____
Solve the Problem
Do Not Interrupt
Do Not Call Each Other Names
Tell the Truth

Ask What Happened Repeat the Problem
What Can You Do to Solve the Problem?
Would This Solve the Problem for *you?*
What Can Be Done Differently?
Both People Must Agree.
Tell Friends that the Problem Has Been Solved.

PART II: ROLE-PLAYING: PRACTICE MAKES PERFECT

SESSION #4

Role-Playing

Conflict Examples

ROLE-PLAYING: MAXIMIZING ITS EFFECTIVENESS

You will now be entering the second phase, in which children will put their knowledge to use by role-playing. Remember your job as the trainer is to facilitate the sessions. Try and act as their "coach." There is no right or wrong way to do this. You want to create an environment where even the shyest of kids isn't embarrassed to go up front. Laughter and "we all make mistakes, even me" is the best way to accomplish this. Even if a child forgets the script or the steps, gently stop the role-play and ask the children watching for their help. Always end each role-play on a positive note: "Didn't they do a wonderful job?" and "Let's give them a round of applause." This makes it easier for the next time.

Also make sure that you switch children playing Problem Kids and Mediators so everyone has a turn to be the Mediators and not just the children with problems. This is very important. Also, when children play Problem Kids, it's a good idea to give them a fictitious names (not a name of someone actually in the class).

Once children learn these skills in make-believe situations, they will be able to apply them in real-life mediations. But it takes time. Remind students that when they were learning to ride a bicycle or roller-skate, they had to practice. Let them gently know in order to become good at mediation, they have to practice too.

ROLE-PLAYING

OBJECTIVE: To teach children about role-playing and how it can help them become successful Mediators.

EXPLANATION: Tell the class: "Role-playing is when we make-believe in imaginary situations so we can practice for real-life situations. We are going to role-play make-believe concepts, but ones that could actually happen in real life." Two children will be the Mediators, and two children will be the Problem Kids.

NOTE TO TEACHERS: Appendix III includes 50 conflict situations to choose from. For the first role-play, let's run through it step-by-step:

Remember to keep the Mediator Clue Cards in a visible place. Let children playing Mediators bring The Mediator Script from their handbooks with them to refer to during the first sessions role-playing. During the later sessions, see if children can run through the steps without referring to The Mediator Script but just from looking at the Mediator Clue Cards.

CONFLICT EXAMPLE: Bud and Mary are partners in a science project. Mary thinks she is doing all the work. The science project is of the solar system, showing all the planets and the moons around Earth, Mars, Jupiter, Saturn, Neptune, and Uranus. Mary has been working every day after school. Often, Bud doesn't show up and makes an excuse. Bud says Mary is a pain. The idea for the solar system project was his idea, and he has other things to do after school, like playing basketball with his friends. Mary and Bud are involved in a shouting match, calling each other nasty names in class. The Mediators are assigned the case.

1. Invite two children to play Mary and Bud acting out the conflict. Name-calling should not involve profanity. They can call each other "stupid," "silly," "nerd."

2. Ask two kids to play the Mediators who know The Mediator Script very well. Watch the complete mediation.

3. Mediator 1 and 2 ask Mary and Bud to agree to the four rules.

   1. Do you both agree to solve the problem?
   2. Do you both agree not to interrupt?
   3. Do you both agree not to call each other names?
   4. Do you both agree to tell the truth?

4. Mary and Bud agree. The Mediators follow the script, asking Mary to tell her side of the story. (Sometimes when role-playing, the children may need a little coaching. If they do, you can suggest, but they should try and improvise themselves and have fun.)

Mary says, "I am doing all the work on this project and it is not fair."

5. Now Bud tells his side of the story.

"She's always on my case. It was my idea anyway."

6. Mediator 1 asks Mary, "What can you do to solve your part of the problem?"

Mary says, "I can say I'm sorry that I called him a jerk. But honestly, I don't think he's doing his fair share."

7. Mediator 2 asks Bud, "What can you say or do to solve your part of the problem?"

Bud says, "I can work out a compromise where we work on the project three days a week, and I promise to keep to the schedule."

8. Mediator 1 asks Mary, "Will this solve the problem for you?" Mary says, "Yes, if he really sticks to it."

9. Mediator 2 asks Bud, "Will this solve the problem for you?" Bud says, "Yes, I will agree to work on the project three days. How about Monday, Wednesday, and Friday? Then Tuesday and Thursday I can play basketball with my friends."

10. Mediator 1 asks, "What can you do if the problem happens again?" Mary says, "I can come to a Mediator and ask for help instead of getting angry and calling him nasty names."

11. Mediator 2 asks Bud the same question. Bud says, "We can try and work out a compromise and talk it out instead of arguing."

12. Mediators congratulate both kids for solving their program and say, "Tell your friends that the problem has been solved so they don't continue talking about it."

After the role-playing, ask the students participating: "What did you think about your role in today's activity? Was there anything you would do differently? What do you think could have been better? What do you think you need to work on?"

After each role-play, ask the class:

What was the Problem Kids' conflict?
How did the Mediators help?
How did the Problem Kids feel at the beginning of the mediation?
How did the Problem Kids feel at the end of the mediation?
Was the problem solution satisfactory for both Problem Kids?
How will they prevent it from happening again?

Try another one: The class can also make up examples or give actual conflicts they've seen or been involved in.

CONFLICT EXAMPLES

Janice can't find her new gold pen. It was a special gift from her favorite aunt. She sees Melissa with a pen that looks just like hers and grabs it. Furious, Melissa pushes Janice. A fight is about to break out. The teacher breaks it up and has Janice and Melissa cool off. She asks the Mediators if they can help Janice and Melissa solve their problem nonviolently.

Sandy had a fight with her best friend, Suzie, and told Peter about it. Later she finds out Peter told the whole school and exaggerated, saying Sandy is so upset she was crying like a little baby. Sandy says Peter has a big mouth and she is going to get her big sister to beat him up and teach him a lesson once and for all.

James is the shortest kid at school. Jerry makes fun of him, calling him a mean name. James gets mad and to get even puts a sign on Jerry's back that says, "NERD." Everyone laughs. James says it serves him right since he was just getting even. The teacher asks the Mediators for help.

Encourage the children to make up some fun examples of their own. Pick familiar ones to which kids can relate. Have the class give the group a round of applause for participating in the exercise.

SESSION #5

Mediator Suggestions

Go over Mediator Suggestions and then continue to Role-Play with the Conflict Examples from Appendix 3 (or use real examples from the class).

MEDIATOR SUGGESTIONS

OBJECTIVES: To teach children that sometimes Mediators will have to give Problem Kids suggestions on how to solve the conflict and teach children how to come up with suggestions that can resolve problems peacefully.

MATERIALS: My Mediator Handbook Sheet #8 - Mediator Suggestions. Point of View Pictures (pages 44 & 45)

WARM-UP: Tell children: "Sometimes people have conflicts because they see things differently." Show them the picture of the Old Woman or Young Woman. Ask, "How many people see the young beautiful woman with the hat?" (Most of them will.) "How many people see the old woman?" Have someone come up and point out the old woman. Do the same with the vase or faces picture.

EXPLANATION: Tell the class, "Sometimes when people see things differently it is hard for them to find a solution to their problem. The Mediators must help them."

PROCEDURES: 1. Use the following conflict or have kids make up their own. Ask two kids to play the roles of Joannie and Cynthia. Have two children play the Mediators.

Cynthia's Point of View: Cynthia wants to play after school with Joannie. But Joannie is always playing double dutch with some girls who live in her building. Cynthia is angry that Joannie is ignoring her lately and playing with the other girls. In front the other girls, Cynthia calls Joannie a nasty name.

Joannie's Point of View: There is a big contest for the best double dutch jump rope group. The winners get to go to Disneyland. Joannie has to practice hard every day. She wants to play with Cynthia, but Cynthia is really bad at double dutch rope, and if she includes her, she feels they might lose the contest. Joannie calls Cynthia a nasty name back and pushes her. The Mediators are called in to help:

2. Go through all the steps of role-playing up to the time when the Mediators ask both Problem Kids what they can say or do to solve their part of the problem.

Have everyone freeze. Ask the class for suggestions:

Here are a few:

1. Walk away from each other.
2. Cool off.
3. Stop calling names.
4. Agree to keep feet and hands to yourself.

3. Ask the class: "After they are cooled off, what are some ways they can work this problem out?" (Joannie can promise that after the contest, she'll spend time with Cynthia; Cynthia can practice jump rope so maybe next time she can be included; Joannie and Cynthia can agree that right now they need to stay away from each other.)

4. Hand out "My Mediator Handbook" Sheet #8. Explain to the children that often in a mediation, both children may decide not to be friends for awhile and that's okay. Then ask: "What is not okay?" (Tip: Not okay to call names, hurt someone or make threats just because your point of view is different.)

5. Go around the room, and have the children read the Mediator Suggestions.

Take a conflict from the Conflict Examples (Appendix 3) and break children into groups of four. (If you have an extra child, they can be an observer.)

6. Two children play the Mediators and two the Problem Kids. Remind the Problem Kids to pretend not to know how to solve the problem when the mediator asks, "What can you say or do to solve your part of the problem?"

Sharing: Have the children go home and share what they learned about Mediator Suggestions with a family member.

MY MEDIATOR HANDBOOK SHEET #8
MEDIATOR SUGGESTIONS

1. Walk away.
2. Stay away from each other.
3. Agree to keep hands, feet, and objects to yourself.
4. Cool off first, then talk to a Mediator.
5. Talk to an adult.
6. Stop calling names.
7. Stop insulting your loved ones.
8. Stop threatening.
9. Give back what was borrowed.
10. Give back what you took away.
11. Leave you alone.
12. Stop blaming.
13. Stop bossing you around.
14. Stop bothering you.
15. Share with you.
16. Stop lying.
17. Stop taking things without asking.
18. Stop spreading rumors or being a tattletale.
19. Don't talk to you, or make mean faces at you.

From role-playing you may come up with your own:

20. _____

21. _____

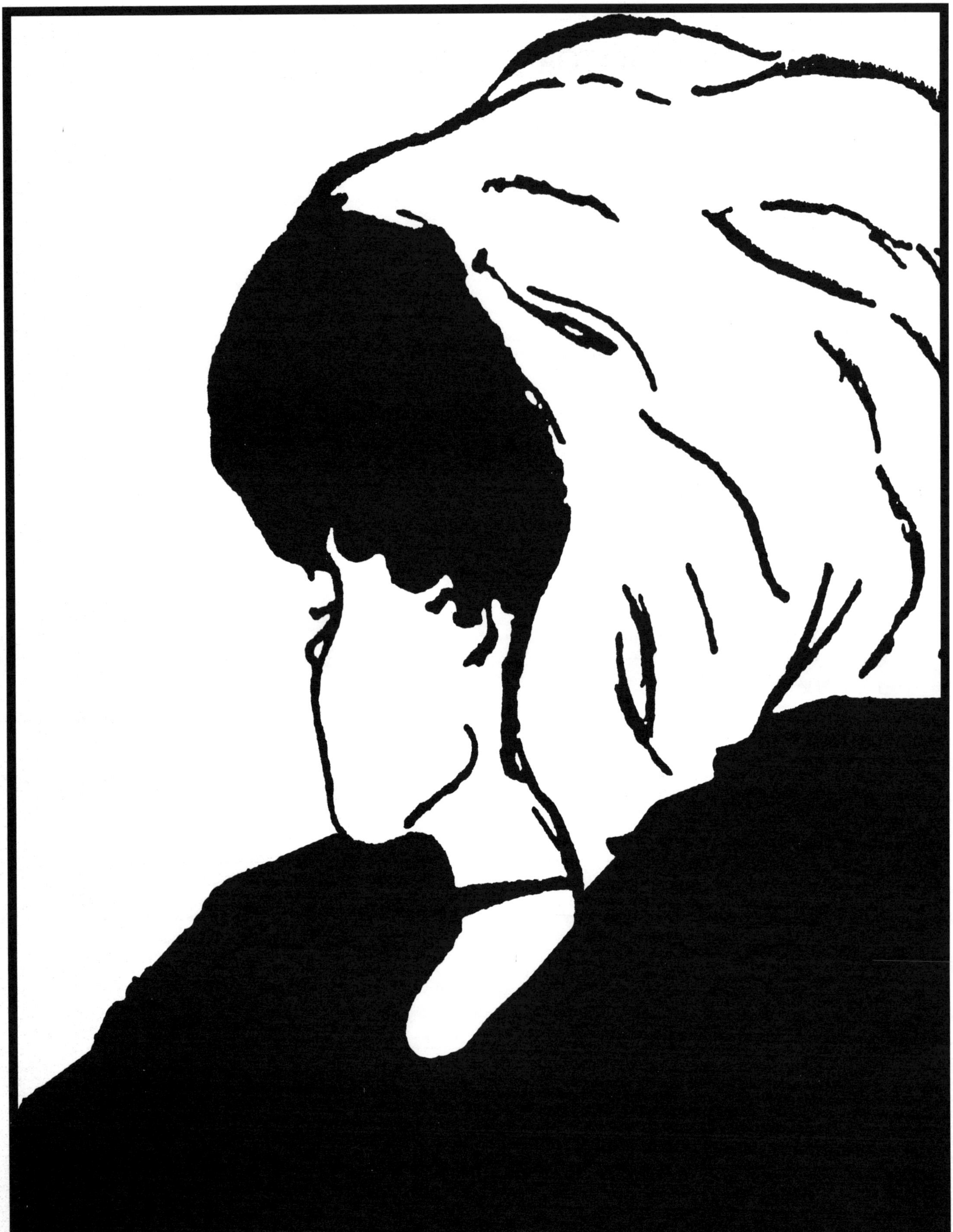

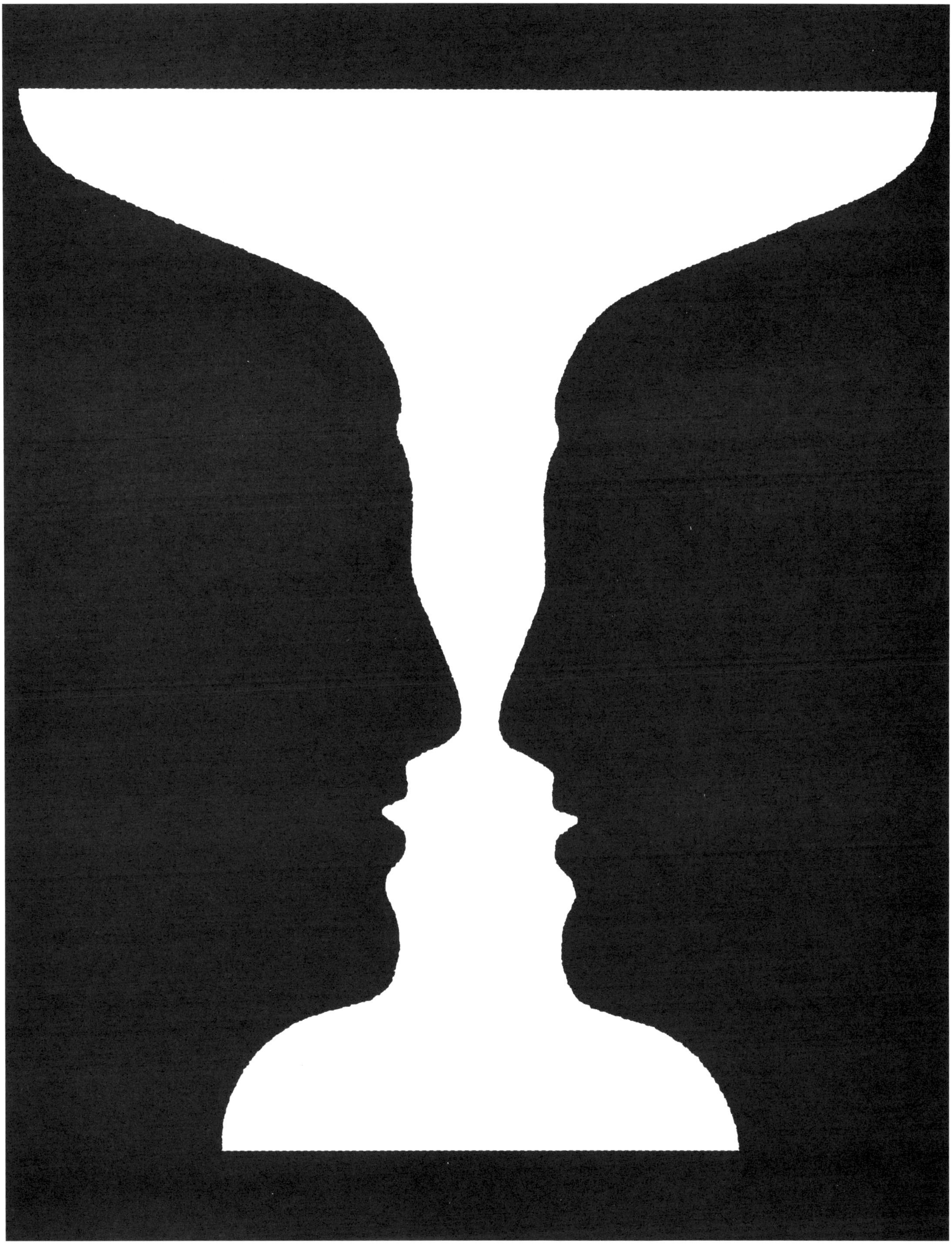

SESSION #6

Handling Objections

Go over Handling Objections and then continue to Role-Play with the Conflict Examples from Appendix 3 (or use real examples from the class).

HANDLING OBJECTIONS

OBJECTIVE: To teach children that there are times when some Problem Kids can make it a little more difficult to solve a problem, and knowing how to handle objections prepares you to handle these times.

MATERIALS: "My Mediator Handbook" Sheet #9 - Handling Objections.

EXPLANATION: When the Mediator says "What can you say or do to solve your part of the problem?" sometimes a Problem Kid may say (s)he's going to beat the other Problem Kid up, or sometimes a Problem Kid may call the other Problem Kid a nasty name. The Mediators have to be prepared and know what to say and do.

PROCEDURE: 1. Call two children up to the front of the room to be the Problem Kids, Kenny and Victor. Have two children pretend to be the Mediators.

CONFLICT: Kenny and Victor were best friends but last week they were playing basketball and had a fight. Kenny says Victor "elbowed him." Kenny is really mad at Victor. During class, he throws a spitball at him and everyone laughs. Victor bops Kenny over the head. The teacher asks the classroom Mediators for help after the boys cool off.

2. Have the children role-play the conflict (but only improvise the bopping over the head). When the Mediator asks Kenny, "What can you do to solve your part of the problem?", he should say, "Get my big brother to beat Victor up."

Ask them to FREEZE. Ask the class: "What do you think the Mediator could say?" (Tip: "We want to solve the problem without making a threat. What can you say or do to solve your part of the problem without making a threat?")

3. Have the children continue the mediation. Explain that this was an example of handling an objection. Hand out "My Mediator Handbook" Sheet #9.
Go around the room and have the children read the objections and discuss.

4. Pick a Conflict Example from Appendix 3 and role-play again, practicing handling objections. Students should refer to their Mediator Handling Objections sheet.

MY MEDIATOR HANDBOOK SHEET #9
HANDLING OBJECTIONS

WHAT TO SAY WHEN KIDS DISAGREE WITH THE MEDIATORS

When a Problem Kid takes too long to explain his side of the story...

Mediators say, "Could you please keep it short?"

When a Problem Kid says, "He called me stupid," or any other name...

Mediators say (repeating), "You're saying he called you a name?"
(Mediators do not repeat the bad name the disputant said.)

When Mediators feel the Problem Kids aren't cooled off...

Mediators say, "Can you both agree to stay away from each other now and come back when you are both cooled off?"

When a Problem Kid makes a threat by saying he will get an older friend or family member to beat up the other kid...

Mediators say, "What can you say or do to solve the problem without threatening or without hurting anybody?"

When a Problem Kid says, "Throw the other kid out of the school or class," or something else that cannot be done by the Mediators...

Mediators say, "We can't do that. What can you say or do together to solve the problem?"

When someone answers, "Tell the teacher..."

Mediators say, "How can you solve the problem between the two of you without an adult?"

When a Problem Kid doesn't want to say "I'm sorry" to solve the problem...

Mediators say, "What else can you do to solve the problem now?"

When a Problem Kid doesn't want a Mediator's suggestions...

Mediators say, "What do you need the other kid to do to solve the problem?"

When a Problem Kid will not stop talking about the problem...

Mediators say, "What can you do from now on to solve the problem?"

When a Problem Kid calls a Mediator a name or hits a Mediator...

Mediators walk away and tell an adult.

If one Mediator forgets what to say in the script...

The other Mediator can say it.

SESSION #7

Mediator's Discipline

Go over Mediator's Discipline and then continue Role-Playing with the Conflict Examples from Appendix 3 (or use real examples from the class).

MEDIATOR'S DISCIPLINE

Children should be informed that Mediators can be disciplined for fighting or other serious problems. They can be suspended from their position as Mediator as well as be terminated from the classroom mediation program. Here is a three-step discipline approach.

First offense: A warning. (Talk to the Mediator and remind him/her of the proper behavior for Mediators.

Second offense: The Mediator is dropped for two weeks from his or her day of duty on the class mediator schedule.

Third offense: The Mediator is removed from the program for the remainder of the school year.

SESSION #8

Mediator's Quiz

Picking the Classroom Mediators

How to Enhance the Program

Continue role-playing from Conflict Examples. Some teachers like to give a "Mediators Quiz;" however, there are children who get nervous taking quizzes so instead of making it a "test," you can review the quiz as a classroom exercise.

You can photocopy the following page and use it as a quiz or a classroom exercise.

Answers to Mediator Quiz:

1. False
2. False
3. True
4. True
5. False
6. False
7. False
8. False
9. False
10. False
11. False
12. True
13. False
14. True
15. False
16. True

MEDIATOR'S QUIZ (Optional)

TRUE OR FALSE (Put a check in the correct box).

		True	False
1.	Mediators are like police. A part of their job is to break up fights.	[ ]	[ ]
2.	When both kids are angry you mediate immediately.	[ ]	[ ]
3.	If two students do not want to solve their problem with the Mediators, you take them to a teacher.	[ ]	[ ]
4.	Mediators give suggestions to kids only when the kids cannot find their own solution.	[ ]	[ ]
5.	A Mediator should tell a Problem Kid to cool off by running up and down the halls.	[ ]	[ ]
6.	Mediators always ask witnesses to tell what happened first.	[ ]	[ ]
7.	Sometimes you have to force kids to solve their problems.	[ ]	[ ]
8.	Problem Kids have to follow the suggestions the Mediators give. [ ]	[ ]	
9.	Mediators should take sides.	[ ]	[ ]
10.	Mediators never decide who speaks first.	[ ]	[ ]
11.	Mediators never ask the Problem Kids their names.	[ ]	[ ]
12.	When both kids are calm, the Mediators decide who speaks first.	[ ]	[ ]
13.	If a Mediator gets in a fight, (s)he can't be suspended.	[ ]	[ ]
14.	If one Mediator forgets what to say in the script, the other Mediator can say it.	[ ]	[ ]
15.	When a Problem Kid is taking too long to tell his side of the story, a Mediator just waits until he finishes.	[ ]	[ ]
16.	When a Problem Kid will not stop talking about the problem, a Mediator says, "What can you do right now to solve the problem?"	[ ]	[ ]

PICKING THE MEDIATORS

As discussed previously, the students must have the qualities of Mediators.

Qualities of Mediators:

1. Well-Behaved
2. Good Listener
3. Ability to Memorize the Mediator Script

If desired, Mediators can wear buttons or a sash to distinguish them. You will post the Classroom Mediator's Schedule (Appendix 2). There should be two to four Mediators on schedule per day. (Many times you can get a grant from a company to give you money for the purchase of Mediator tee-shirts.) This is, of course, optional.

children can write notes as to why they want to be picked as a mediator. (This is optional.) If desired you can hand out the form in Appendix 1 to students. When chosen, congratulate the classroom Mediators. Tell the other students that perhaps next time they can become classroom Mediators.

If you'd like, you can have the Mediators bring in a picture of themselves or you can take pictures of the mediators and for that day put their picture on the board.

Students chosen as Mediators should receive a Parent Note Home and a Mediator Certificate. From time to time, for their service, you may want to treat them to a special lunch. Some teachers invite the mediators to have lunch with them during the lunch hour when the other students go to the cafeteria. Many teachers bring a special dessert or treat. During these times, you can informally chat about the successes of the program and how they feel it could be improved. They can discuss special problems with you. Often teachers learn the most about how the program is working from these informal meetings. It also gives the Mediators a sense of reward for their hard work and dedication.

HOW TO ENHANCE THE PROGRAM

Buttons, sashes or vests can be worn by the Mediators. Buttons are the least expensive. Sashes can be made by parents or bought. Vests can also be bought inexpensively. You only need four and maybe some back-ups if they get lost during the year.

You can buy a small amplifier and four microphones for the children to use when they come to the front of the room to role-play. This is a minimal cost. You can also apply for many small grants to purchase this equipment. Explain in the grant that you have begun a mediation program to teach children nonviolent ways to handle conflicts. You have a good chance of obtaining funding for the amp and microphones.

HOW OTHER SCHOOL PERSONNEL CAN HELP

As a guidance counselor, I was interested in helping the teachers at my school begin this program, so I lent my support and my time. If you have a guidance counselor or other licensed school personnel who can assist you, you can speed up the time it will take to train your class.

When you are training your class, and the children are at the role-playing stage, the guidance counselor or other trained person can take four students with him or her to role-play. Two students will be Mediators and two will be Problem Kids. Reverse the roles to give all four students a chance to be Mediators. Return the four students to the classroom and take four more. Repeat. An additional 8-12 students can be trained in a 40-minute period if you have assistance.

Many teachers find it helpful for students to give them a Teacher Report Card (see Appendix 1). This can give you the best feedback. Children should remain anonymous. Remember the old saying: "We are all teachers and pupils of each other." Many times our pupils are our best teachers.

PART III: GETTING PARENTS INVOLVED

Bringing Mediation and Conflict Resolution Home

De-Stressing Tips for Parents

De-Stressing Common Sense

Help! My Kids Are Driving Me Crazy!

Cool-Off Zones

Anger Management Activities

BRINGING MEDIATION AND CONFLICT RESOLUTION HOME

Children have a tendency to emulate their parent's behavior. The way their mothers and fathers handle frustrations and control their anger will greatly influence how children settle disagreements.

For many children this will mean they will be getting double messages. At home, they may be seeing their parents handle conflicts in hurtful ways. As we know all too well, often our most destructive conflicts are with people we love very much. At school, they will be learning positive and constructive ways to deal with conflicts. For some children, they may need to discuss their feelings about these "double messages" with you or their guidance counselor.

If your school has open school week or regular PTA meetings, you may want to demonstrate mediation to parents using your best Mediators. You may also have some children who have had problems talk about how mediation helped them.

All people, not just children, need these skills. Most parents will be deeply indebted to you for showing them ways to make their own homes and lives more peaceful.

DE-STRESSING TIPS FOR PARENTS

1. Count to 10 and recite the alphabet forward or backward.

2. Take deep breaths.

3. Think about a peaceful or relaxing place.

4. Take a hot bubble bath.

5. Listen to your favorite music.

6. Punch a pillow.

7. Hug yourself.

8. Talk to yourself in positive ways. Don't make things worse by negative self talk. ("I am calming down, I feel better now. All the tension is leaving my body.")

9. Go for a jog.

10. Look at nature.

11. Smile at a neighbor.

12. Call a friend.

13. Keep an anger journal and write what you feel.

14. Tell yourself a joke.

15. Ask yourself: "If someone else had this problem, what would I tell him or her to do?"

The next time I feel totally stressed and feel like taking it out on someone close to me, I will:

_____

_____

_____

_____

DE-STRESSING COMMON SENSE

1. **Treat yourself "first class".** That means doing what you know in your heart is best for you. Eat balanced meals. Avoid too much sugar, caffeine, or fatty foods. These can make stress worse.

2. **Take a little time just for yourself.** Find a book you like and give yourself permission to read one chapter after dinner all alone (or even one page or paragraph). Do something you like to do, such as planting a garden, writing a poem, or drawing a picture.

3. **Get involved in a good exercise program,** even if it's just 15-20 minutes a day, and you have to wake up a little earlier. Try something you like; don't force yourself to do something you don't like to do. Exercise makes the brain release endorphins which make you feel better. (Always consult with your physician before beginning any exercise program.)

4. **Speak in positive affirmations and in the present.** Don't catastrophize. Tell yourself, "I am calming down." "I feel happier now." "I am relaxing." "I'm in control." When a voice says, "This is terrible, this is awful," say "STOP. I'm not listening to you now." Return to the positive affirmation. (When you're calm, come up with your affirmations so you're prepared ahead of time.)

5. **Assert yourself, but after you've calmed down.** When you do, use "I" sentences. Instead of saying, "You make me so unhappy" or "You don't understand," speak in "I" sentences. Say, "I feel unhappy when you (cite behavior)." "You" sentences cast blame on the other person. "I" sentences put you in control. When disciplining children, let them know that it is their behavior you don't like, but you will always love them. It works with big people too. Sometimes just prefacing a confrontation with "I love you" dissolves tensions and works miracles.

"I love you Kevin, but I feel angry when you leave your toys all over the house."
"I love you, honey, but I feel upset when you're late and you don't call."

HELP! MY KIDS ARE DRIVING ME CRAZY!

When Siblings Fight

If children cannot solve a problem by themselves, you can step in as a "Parent Mediator." Becoming a Parent Mediator is a very effective way to help your children (and their friends or relatives) solve problems.

When you act as a Parent Mediator, you need to be neutral. If one of your children thinks you are taking sides, it will not work.

Before acting as a Parent Mediator, make sure both children are cooled off. If not, send them to their Cool-Off Zones (see next page).

The Parent as Mediator

Preface: Say, "I am not going to take sides."

1. Ask: "What is the problem?" Ask the angriest child to tell his (her) side of the story first.
2. After each child speaks, repeat what they've told you in your own words.
3. Ask: "What are some ways to solve the problem?" Try not to give your suggestions. See if they can come up with their own.
4. When they decide on a solution, repeat what the solution is. "So, as I understand it you will share the paint set. So as I understand it, you will take turns with the basketball."
5. Ask: "If this happens again, what will you do?"
6. Congratulate them for solving their problem. Reinforce, "I am very proud of you for solving the problem. I knew you could do it."

When They Are Too Hot to Handle

When children are very angry, send them to their Cool-Off Zones immediately.

1. Instead of asking: "What's going on here?" immediately separate the children.
2. Say: "You are too angry to be together. Go to your Cool-Off Zones now."
3. After both children have gone to their Cool-Off Zones, visit them.
   Ask: "Do you think you are calmed down enough to solve the problem with _____?"
4. If they say yes, go through the mediation, having them both tell their side of the story.

COOL-OFF ZONES

Cool-Off Zones are the most important way to keep conflicts from turning physically ugly. This works extremely well with adults too. When a conflict develops where there is a lot of anger, each person will go to his or her Cool-Off Zone. There will be no attempt to work on solving a problem until everyone is cooled off and calmed down. Before working on a problem, ask both people if they are honestly cooled off. Tell them they must tell the truth.

You will be amazed at how much easier it is to solve a problem when both people involved are calmed down and able to think clearly. In the heat of anger, people (including children) say and do things they feel badly about afterwards. By cooling off first, everyone wins.

Here's how it works:

At a time when everyone is calm, decide where each person's cool-off area (zone) will be. Agree that each person involved in the dispute will stay there for about 30 minutes. No one is allowed to talk during this time. After 30 minutes is up, and everyone involved is calm, the problem can be discussed. If one of the people involved is not cooled off, take another 30-minute break.

This is not only good for children but for spouses as well. You may want to have Cool-Off Zones for you and your partner. Remember, even though it is so tempting to "yell" when you are mad, it is worth the while to go to your Cool-Off Zone and calm down. Since we teach what we demonstrate, your children will see you seeking an alternative way to solve family conflicts and they will be inclined to follow in your footsteps.

ANGER MANAGEMENT ACTIVITIES

As you start to readjust your temper barometers, you will be able to manage your own anger better. If "one" is very peaceful and "ten" is the angriest you have ever been, you can get a feel where your temper barometer is anytime you do not feel centered. Here are some ways to lower your temperature barometer.

YOGI BREATHE

The yogis believe that the breath is "prana" or life force. By breathing in a special way, you can actually calm yourself down. Here's how: Stand straight. Take a deep breath through your nose and hold it. As you hold it feel it sinking down into your lungs. Your stomach will extend like a balloon. Now exhale though your mouth, feeling all the air leave the balloon slowly.

LOOSEN-UP

Lie in a comfortable chair. Tighten the muscles in your right leg. Hold the tension for a minute. Then shake the leg and feel the tension slipping away. Say the word aloud, LOOSE. Now tighten the muscles in your left leg. Hold the tension for a few moments and feel the tension slipping away. Repeat with your right and left arm. Tense your neck, face, shoulders, stomach, buttocks and then feel the tension slipping away.

"MY FAVORITE PLACE"

Take a vacation with your mind. Close your eyes. Imagine a place you have been or would like to visit. Really visualize it. If it is by the water, imagine that you can feel some drops of water splash you. If it is a sunny day, feel the hot sun on your face. See the colors vividly. Hear the sounds, perhaps the ocean crashing, a bird singing, a musical band playing your favorite song. Smell the air. Breathe in all the love in the world. Breathe out all the fear, tensions, hate, and resentments. Breathe in all the peace. Breathe out all the problems. Open your eyes and feel refreshed.

MEDITATE

Sit in a chair comfortably. Close your eyes. Relax.

Select a word that you can say to yourself that calms you ("calm," "peace," "one," "relax," etc.).

Say the word over and over. Do not let other thoughts interrupt. If they do, say, "Go away. This is my special time now. I will think about you later." Then refocus your breathing and say your special word again.

When you are in a "difficult situation," try and say your special word to yourself and monitor your reaction.

WORRIES AWAY

Sit in a comfortable chair or lie down. Imagine your worries. See the worries falling into a river of water. Imagine the problem being carried away by a current. See yourself standing by the bank of the river. You are smiling, peaceful, and calm. Quiet your mind. Before you open your eyes, tell yourself, "I feel positive and confident that I can handle anything. When I open my eyes, I will feel renewed and refreshed."

You can improvise or create your own "mental exercises" for helping yourself calm down.

APPENDIX 1

WHY I WANT TO BE A CLASSROOM MEDIATOR

Name: _____

Class: _____

I would make an excellent Classroom Mediator because:

_____
_____
_____
_____

At school, when I have a problem, I

_____
_____
_____
_____

At home, when I have a problem, I

_____
_____
_____
_____

I like to help people. At school, I help by:

_____
_____
_____
_____

At home, I help by:

_____
_____
_____
_____

Have you memorized The Mediator Script? Circle one.   **Yes**   **No**

TEACHER'S REPORT CARD

You do not have to fill in your name.

I liked being trained as a Classroom Mediator. I learned many things about solving problems. One of the most important things I learned was:

_____

_____

_____

The part that I did not like about the training was: (optional)

_____

_____

_____

To make the training better, if I was the teacher, I would:

_____

_____

_____

MEDIATOR CERTIFICATE

AWARDED TO

_____

IN RECOGNITION OF YOUR OUTSTANDING MEDIATION SKILLS & HELP IN CREATING A MORE PEACEFUL SCHOOL

DATE: _____

SIGNED:

_____

SIGNED:

_____

CLASS MEDIATOR SCHEDULE

WEEK A

MONDAY	TUESDAY	WEDNESDAY	THURSDAY	FRIDAY

WEEK B

MONDAY	TUESDAY	WEDNESDAY	THURSDAY	FRIDAY

APPENDIX 2

MEDIATOR'S CLASSROOM CONFLICT REPORT FORM

Name of Mediator: _____
Problem Kid Names: _____
and _____

The problem was (describe in one or two sentences):

_____
_____
_____
_____

Problem Kid #1 agreed to:

_____
_____
_____
_____

Problem Kid #2 agreed to:

_____
_____
_____
_____

Circle One

The problem was solved

The problem was not solved

Circle One

The Problem Kids are now friendly toward each other.

The Problem kids agreed to stay away from one another.

Date: _____

Preliminary Parent Letter

Dear Parent or Guardian:

Our class is beginning a mediation program. We are learning how to solve classroom problems peacefully. Your child may come home with some sharing assignments in which (s)he will be sharing what (s)he is learning about mediation with you and asking you what you think about important skills. I thank you for helping your child learn these invaluable techniques, which I believe will give them a better understanding and appreciation of solving conflicts in constructive and creative ways.

Thank you.

Parent Letter: Congratulations Mediators

Dear Parent or Guardian:

Your child has been chosen as a classroom Mediator. A Mediator is a child who helps other children find creative ways to solve problems. Your child completed an eight-week program in which (s)he demonstrated leadership abilities.

I am very proud of _____, and I am sure you are too. Please have your child bring in a photo. When (s)he is on duty, we will post the photo on the bulletin board.

Best wishes,

APPENDIX 3

SAMPLE ROLE-PLAYS FOR MEDIATION
(Assume all conflicts can turn into fights.)

You can use these, improvise on them, create your own, or ask the children to come up with conflicts real or made up.

1. Student A pushes in front of Student B while (s)he is waiting to drink from the water fountain.
2. Student A borrows Student B's favorite pencil and loses it.
3. Student A borrows a quarter from Student B and doesn't pay him or her back.
4. Student A accidentally knocks a carton of milk off of Student B's lunch tray.
5. Student A knocks Student B's coat down in the closet and doesn't pick it up.
6. Student A calls Student B's mother a name.
7. Student A calls Student B a name.
8. Student A threatens to get his big brother to beat Student B up after school.
9. Student A takes Student B's ball away from him or her.
10. Student A grabs Student B's pencil and breaks it.
11. Student A is spreading rumors that Student B cheated on a test.
12. Student A spreads a rumor that Student B is not good in sports.
13. Student A knocks Student B's notebook off his or her desk.
14. Student A tells a lie about Student B.
15. Student A takes Student B's cupcake while (s)he is not looking.
16. Student A keeps talking to Student B in class while (s)he is trying to pay attention to the teacher.
17. Student A pushes Student B out of his/her chair.
18. Student A ruins Student B's computer game while (s)he's in the middle of it.
19. Student A finds Student B's pencil and says it's his or hers.
20. Student A throws Student B's book on the floor in the library.
21. Student A grabs a book out of Student B's hands in the library.

22. Student A takes Student B's hat in the yard and starts throwing it around.

23. Student A trips Student B and doesn't say sorry.

24. Student A tagged Student B too hard while they were playing tag.

25. Student A lets Student B hold his or her game and the teacher takes it away.

26. Student A asks Student B for his or her snack, and Student B gives it to someone else.

27. Student A pushes Student B, and (s)he falls while they are playing basketball.

28. Student A erases some of Student B's work on the computer by accident.

29. Student A promises to play with Student B and then plays with someone else.

30. Student A tells a friend a secret about Student B, and Student B is very upset because (s)he asked Student A not to tell anyone.

31. Student A cheats while Student B is playing a game with him or her.

32. Student A promises to eat lunch with Student B and sits with someone else.

33. Student A grabs Student B's juice and opens it.

34. Student A is swinging her (his) arms in the lunch line and hits Student B.

35. Student A hits Student B and says someone else did it.

36. Student A play fights with someone else and accidentally knocks into Student B.

37. Student A borrows Student B's game and forgets to bring it back the next day.

38. Student A, who is bigger than Student B, asks Student B to carry his or her books for him or her.

39. Student A pushes Student B off the lunch line, and (s)he loses his or her place.

40. Student A wants to sit in the same chair as Student B.

41. Student A always gets Student B in trouble, and Student B doesn't want to sit next him or her.

42. Student A wants Student B to carry another kid's books in his or her book bag.

43. Student A jumps on Student B's back and hurts him or her.

44. Student A starts a rumor that Student B has a crush on someone in class.

45. Student A loses Student B's library book.

46. Student A threatens to get his or her big brother to hurt Student B after school because Student B didn't return a basketball (s)he borrowed.

47. Student A threatens to have a gang of kids beat Student B because (s)he called him or her a name.

48. Student A promised to bring Student B a snack for lunch and forgets.

49. Student A tattles on Student B for not doing his or her homework.

50. Student A skips Student's B's turn when they are playing a game with some other kids in the yard.

ABOUT THE AUTHORS

Max Nass, M.S. is an elementary peer mediation trainer and guidance counselor. He was awarded "Outstanding Performance in the Field of Counseling" from the New York City Association for Counseling & Development for his "Mediation For Little Peacemakers" (previously titled "Whole Class Mediation") and "Songs For Peacemakers" conflict resolution programs.

Mr. Nass has appeared on *The Oprah Winfrey Show,* Fox-TV's *Good Day-New York,* Cable News Network, *The McCreary Report, Eyewitness News, Real News for Kids* and ABC's *Making A Difference.* In addition, he has been a guest on radio shows throughout the United States and Canada.

He lectures frequently and conducts workshops for teachers, community leaders, parents and kids on mediation and conflict resolution. Mr. Nass has been the recipient of numerous awards and grants for recognition of his work in bringing about more peaceful schools and communities. He is a former elementary school teacher.

Marcia Nass is a journalist who assists her husband in workshop presentations to teachers and parents. Ms. Nass has won numerous grants on behalf of inner-city children and their families. She is co-author of the award-winning *Songs For Peacemakers* program.

Articles on Mr. and Mrs. Nass and their programs have appeared in *The New York Times, The Daily News, The Boston Parent's Paper, Long Island Parenting, Newsday, Teaching Tolerance, The United Federation of Teachers Newsletter, The American Federation of Teachers Newsletter* and *Essence Magazine.*